modern readers — stage 1

The Flood

Eduardo Amos
Elisabeth Prescher
Ernesto Pasqualin

Richmond

© EDUARDO AMOS, ELISABETH PRESCHER, ERNESTO PASQUALIN, 2004

Richmond

Diretoria: *Paul Berry*
Gerência editorial: *Sandra Possas*
Coordenação de bureau: *Américo Jesus*
Coordenação de revisão: *Estevam Vieira Lédo Jr.*
Coordenação de produção gráfica: *André Monteiro, Maria de Lourdes Rodrigues*
Coordenação de produção industrial: *Wilson Troque*

Projeto editorial: *Véra Regina A. Maselli, Kylie Mackin*

Assistência editorial: *Gabriela Peixoto Vilanova*
Revisão: *Denise Ceron*
Projeto gráfico de miolo e capa: *Ricardo Van Steen Comunicações e Propaganda Ltda./Oliver Fuchs*
Edição de arte: *Christiane Borin*
Ilustrações de miolo e capa: *Lélis*
Tratamento de imagens: *Ideraldo Araújo de Melo*
Diagramação: *EXATA Editoração*
Pré-impressão: *Helio P. de Souza Filho, Marcio H. Kamoto*
Impressão e acabamento: *Coan Indústria Gráfica Ltda.*
Lote: 278434

Dados Internacionais de Catalogação na Publicação (CIP)
(Câmara Brasileira do Livro, SP, Brasil)

Amos, Eduardo.
  The Flood / Eduardo Amos, Elisabeth Prescher,
Ernesto Pasqualin; (ilustrações Lélis). — São
Paulo : Moderna, 2003. — (Modern readers ; stage 1)

  1. Inglês (Ensino fundamental) I. Prescher,
Elisabeth. II. Pasqualin, Ernesto. III. Lélis.
IV. Título. III. Série.

03-3364   CDD-372.652

Índices para catálogo sistemático:
1. Inglês : Ensino fundamental   372.652

ISBN 85-16-03727-4

Reprodução proibida. Art. 184 do Código Penal e Lei 9.610 de 19 de fevereiro de 1998.

Todos os direitos reservados.

RICHMOND
EDITORA MODERNA LTDA.
Rua Padre Adelino, 758 — Belenzinho
São Paulo — SP — Brasil — CEP 03303-904
Central de atendimento ao usuário: 0800 771 8181
www.richmond.com.br
2019

Impresso no Brasil

It is a very hot summer afternoon in Vila Buriti. There are many people in the square because of the Third Interschool Rap Festival. Today is the second day of the festival.

Renata and Rodrigo Macedo are brother and sister. They are twins. Renata is very happy today because her band is a success. Her brother's band is also in the festival.

Mr Macedo, the kids' father, and their school director, Mrs Moreira, are there too.

Mrs Moreira – Hi, kids! Are you ready for the show?

Renata – Oh, yes! We sure are. The festival is exciting and all the students in our neighborhood are here today.

Mr Macedo – How about you, Rodrigo? Aren't you excited too?

Rodrigo – Not really. My band isn't very good.

Mrs Moreira – Cheer up, Rodrigo! You are only a beginner. What about you, Mr Macedo? Are you here to see your kids?

Mr Macedo – No, I'm on duty today. There are many people from other neighborhoods. The fire brigade is here to help the police.

Renata – Rodrigo! There is a garbage can near you. Throw your bottle there!

Rodrigo – Calm down, Renata! It's only a bottle.

The next morning, there are tons of bottles, cans and paper bags in the square. Macedo and Roberto Dantas are there. Dantas is Macedo's friend. He is a policeman.

Mr Macedo – How are things, Dantas?

Mr Dantas – Difficult. There is a lot of trash on the ground. I am worried. Look at the sky!

Mr Macedo – Mmm... It's very dark. Are you afraid of a flood?

Mr Dantas – Yes. I am worried about the houses down the street! Let's call for help!

Dantas is right. A few minutes later, the rain is very heavy in Vila Buriti. Together, a lot of rain and garbage is disastrous. In the streets below, the families are in danger. The level of the water is high. There are people at the windows and on the roofs. The fire brigade and the police are there to help. Macedo and Dantas are in the middle of the flood.

Mr Dantas – Macedo! Macedo! Take this family to the school. Hurry up! The water current is very strong. There are still many people on the roof tops and inside the houses.

Mr Macedo – Is your family in a safe place, Dantas?

Mr Dantas – Yes, they are at the school. How about your wife and kids, Macedo?

Mr Macedo – Julia and the twins are safe. My house is out of the flood area.

An hour later, Mr Macedo is at the school. There are many firefighters and police officers too. And there are many families from the flood area. The young children are frightened and hungry. Their mothers are tired and upset. All their things are still inside the houses.

Mr Macedo – Mrs Moreira! Here are more children. They are from the flood area. They're hungry and cold.

Mrs Moreira – Don't worry, Mr Macedo. There are sandwiches and fruit juice for everyone. How are things in the streets below and near the market?

Mr Macedo – Not good! A lot of people are still there.

Suddenly, ... RIIIINNG... It's Macedo's cell phone.

Mr Macedo — Hello! Julia? ... Yes, I'm fine. What?... The children are not at home with you? They are at Helena's house? ... But it is close to the market! They are in the flood area!

Mr Macedo is back at the flood area. There are many streets underwater now. Many houses are destroyed and many people are hurt. Mr Macedo is in the boat again. He is worried about Rodrigo and Renata.

Dantas — Macedo! Macedo! Quick! Renata and Rodrigo are near the market. They are in the middle of the flood. Hurry up! Follow me!

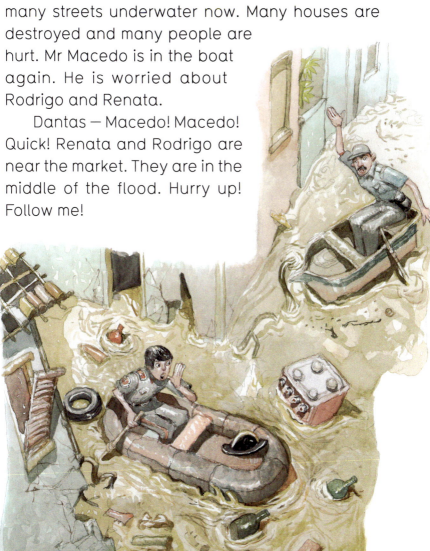

Mr Macedo – Where are they? Where are my kids?

Mr Dantas – Over there, Macedo. On that tree, in the middle of the flood! Look! The girl is on the tree. The boy is in the water.

Mr Macedo – Oh no! The current is too strong there. They are in terrible danger! Let's go, Dantas!

Mr Dantas – No! Stay here! Your men are already there. The situation is under control. Look! They are close to the kids now.

Mr Macedo - I'm afraid. Renata isn't strong and Rodrigo is too tired.

Mr Dantas – Calm down Macedo! Look! Rodrigo is already in the boat. And now, Renata too! They are safe.

One hour later, Rodrigo is in an ambulance. He is too tired to walk. He is very frightened and cold. But he isn't badly hurt. Renata is in shock and very weak. But the rain is finally over.

Mr Macedo – Renata! Rodrigo! Are you OK?

Rodrigo – Yes, Dad. But I'm very tired and cold, very cold.

Mr Macedo – Renata, talk to me! Are you OK?

Mrs Moreira – Look at the kids, Mr Macedo. Aren't you proud of them?

Mr Macedo – I sure am. Their campaign "Put the trash in the can" is a success.

Mrs Moreira – You're right. Today is the last day of the festival and the streets are clean. No bottles, no cans, no paper bags! But look! There are dark clouds in the sky.

Mr Macedo – Are you afraid of the rain, Mrs Moreira?

Mrs Moreira – Not now, Mr Macedo. Not now.

The meaning of each word corresponds to its use in the context of the story (see page number 00)

a lot of (5) muito
afraid of (12) medo de
afternoon (3) tarde
again (9) de novo
also (3) também
back (9) de volta
because (3) porque
beginner (4) iniciante
below (6) abaixo
boat (9) barco
bottle (4) garrafa
brother (3) irmão
campaign (12) campanha
can (5) lata
child, children (8) criança/s
clean (12) limpo
close (10) perto
cloud (12) nuvem
cold (8) frio
current (10) correnteza
danger (6) perigo
dark (5) escuro
destroyed (9) destruído
disastrous (6) desastroso
down (5) abaixo
everyone (8) todos
exciting (4) divertido
family, families (6) família/s
fire brigade (4) corpo de bombeiros

firefighter (8) bombeiro
flood (5) enchente
frightened (11) assustado
garbage can (4) lata de lixo
ground (5) chão
happy (3) feliz
heavy (6) pesado
help (4) ajudar
high (6) alto
hot (3) quente
hour (8) hora
hungry (8) com fome
hurt (9) machucado
inside (7) dentro
kid, kids (4) criança/s
later (8) mais tarde
man, men (10) homem/ns
many (3) muitos
market (8) mercado
middle (10) meio
near (4) perto
neighborhood (4) bairro
next (5) próximo
only (4) apenas
out of (7) fora
paper bag (5) saquinho de papel
people (3) pessoas
place (7) lugar
police officer (8) policial

13

proud (12) orgulhoso
rain (6) chuva
ready (4) pronto
roof, roofs (6) telhado/s
safe (7) seguro
sandwich, sandwiches (8) sanduíche/s
second (3) segundo
sister (3) irmã
sky (5) céu
square (3) praça
stay (10) ficar
still (7) ainda
strong (10) forte
summer (3) verão
sure (4) certamente
take (7) levar
thing (8) coisa
throw (4) atirar
tired (8) cansado
together (6) juntos
tons (5) toneladas
too (4) também
trash (5) lixo
twin, twins (3) gêmeo/s
underwater (9) embaixo d'água

upset (8) nervoso
very (3) muito, bastante
water (10) água
weak (11) fraco
wife (7) esposa
window (6) janela
worried (5) preocupado
young (8) pequeno

Expressions

Calm down! (4) Calma!
Cheer up! (4) Anime-se!
Don't worry! (8) Não se preocupe!
Follow me! (9) Siga-me!
How about you...? (4) E você?
How are things? (5) Como vão as coisas?
Hurry up! (7) Apresse-se!
in shock (11) em estado de choque
Let's go! (10) Vamos!
Not now (12) Agora não
Not really (4) Na realidade não
Over there (10) Lá
Quick! (9) Rápido!
under control (10) sob controle

ACTIVITIES

Before Reading

1. Read the back cover of the book. Look at the picture on the front cover and the title, The Flood.

   Is the story about:
   ( ) music   ( ) a party   ( ) a disaster

2. Look at the pictures on pages 3 and 4. Find these things:

   > paper   a garbage can   bottles   cans

While Reading

Pages 3 and 4

3. Read page 3 and correct these sentences:
   a) It is a hot summer evening.
   b) It is the first day of the Rap Festival.
   c) Renata's band isn't good.

4. Read page 4 and circle the correct answer.
   Renata is angry at Rodrigo because:
   a) his band is a success.
   b) he throws a bottle on the ground.

Pages 5 to 7

5. Before you read on, look at the picture on page 5. What can you see? Complete the sentences.
   a) The sky is ....
   b) There is a lot of .... in the square.

6. Read and check your answers to 5.

15

7. Now read pages 6 and 7 and answer these questions:
   a) Who is in danger? Why?
   b) Who is there to help?
   c) Who is in the middle of the flood?
   d) Who is at the school?

Pages 8 and 9

8. Circle the correct answer:
   a) Mr Macedo is/are at the school.
   b) The streets is/are underwater.
   c) Many houses is/are destroyed.
   d) Mr Macedo's children isn't/aren't at home.

Pages 10 and 11

9. Read and answer:
   a) Who sees the kids?
   b) Who is on the tree?
   c) Who is in the water?
   d) Who is close to the kids?
   e) Who is in an ambulance?

Page 12

10. Before you read, look at the picture on page 12. Look at the picture on page 3.
    What is the same? What is different?

11. Read and answer:
    a) Who is proud of the kids? Why?
    b) Is Mrs Moreira afraid of the rain? Why/Why not?

After Reading (Optional Activities)

12. Are there campaigns in your town/city for the recycling of garbage? Find out about them.

13. Prepare posters for your school about appropriate garbage disposal. Example: "CANS IN THE CAN"